'They wanted me to give a concert; I wanted them to beg me. And so they did. I gave a concert.'

WOLFGANG AMADEUS MOZART
Born 1756, Salzburg
Died 1791, Vienna

This selection of letters between Mozart and his father
was written between October 1777 and July 1778.

MOZART IN PENGUIN CLASSICS
Mozart: A Life in Letters

WOLFGANG AMADEUS MOZART

My Dearest Father

Translated by
Stewart Spencer

PENGUIN BOOKS

PENGUIN CLASSICS

Published by the Penguin Group
Penguin Books Ltd, 80 Strand, London WC2R ORL, England
Penguin Group (USA) Inc., 375 Hudson Street, New York, New York 10014, USA
Penguin Group (Canada), 90 Eglinton Avenue East, Suite 700, Toronto, Ontario,
Canada M4P 2Y3 (a division of Pearson Penguin Canada Inc.)
Penguin Ireland, 25 St Stephen's Green, Dublin 2, Ireland
(a division of Penguin Books Ltd)
Penguin Group (Australia), 707 Collins Street, Melbourne, Victoria 3008, Australia
(a division of Pearson Australia Group Pty Ltd)
Penguin Books India Pvt Ltd, 11 Community Centre, Panchsheel Park,
New Delhi – 110 017, India
Penguin Group (NZ), 67 Apollo Drive, Rosedale, Auckland 0632, New Zealand
(a division of Pearson New Zealand Ltd)
Penguin Books (South Africa) (Pty) Ltd, Block D, Rosebank Office Park,
181 Jan Smuts Avenue, Parktown North, Gauteng 2193, South Africa

Penguin Books Ltd, Registered Offices: 80 Strand, London WC2R ORL, England

www.penguin.com

This selection published in Penguin Classics 2015
001

Translation copyright © Stewart Spencer, 2006
The moral right of the translator has been asserted.

Set in 9.5/13 pt Baskerville 10 Pro
Typeset by Jouve (UK), Milton Keynes
Printed in Great Britain by Clays Ltd, St Ives plc

A CIP catalogue record for this book is available from the British Library

ISBN: 978-0-141-39762-7

www.greenpenguin.co.uk

Mozart to his father,
17 October 1777, Augsburg

Mon très cher Père,

I must start with Stein's pianofortes. Before I saw any of Stein's work, I'd always preferred Späth's pianos; but now I prefer Stein's, as they damp so much better than the Regensburg instruments. If I strike hard, it doesn't matter whether I keep my finger down or raise it, the sound ceases the moment I produce it. However I attack the keys, the tone is always even. It doesn't produce a clattering sound, it doesn't get louder or softer or fail to sound at all; in a word, it's always even. It's true, he won't part with a pianoforte like this for under 300 florins, but the effort and labour that he expends on it can't be paid for. A particular feature of his instruments is their escape action. Not one maker in a hundred bothers with this. But without escape action it's impossible for a pianoforte not to produce a clattering sound or to go on sounding after the note has been struck; when you strike the keys, his hammers fall back again the moment they hit the strings, whether you hold down the keys or release them. He told me that only when he's finished making a piano

1

like this does he sit down and try out all the passagework, runs and leaps, and, using a shave, works away at the instrument until it can do everything. For he works only to serve the music, not just for his own profit, otherwise he'd be finished at once.

He often says that if he weren't such a great music lover and didn't have some slight skill on the instrument, he'd long since have run out of patience with his work; but he loves an instrument that never lets the player down and that will last. His pianos will really last. He guarantees that the sounding board won't break or crack. Once he's finished making a sounding board for a piano he puts it outside, exposing it to the air, rain, snow, heat of the sun and all the devils in order for it to crack, and then he inserts wedges, which he glues in, so that it's very strong and firm. He's perfectly happy for it to crack as he's then assured that nothing more can happen to it. Indeed, he often cuts into it himself and then glues it back together again and makes it really strong. He has completed three such pianofortes. Not until today did I play on one of them again. Today – the 17th – we had lunch with young Herr Gasser, a young and handsome widower who's lost his young and beautiful wife. They'd been married for only 2 years. He's a most excellent and polite young man. We were splendidly entertained. Also there was a colleague of Abbé Henri, Bullinger and Wieshofer, an ex-Jesuit who's now Kapellmeister at the cathedral here. He knows Herr *Schachtner* very well, he was his

choirmaster in Ingolstadt. He's called Pater Gerbl. I'm
to give his best wishes to Herr Schachtner. After lunch
Herr Gasser and I went to Herr *Stein's*, where we were
accompanied by one of his sisters-in-law as well as Mama
and our cousin. At 4 o'clock we were joined by the
Kapellmeister and Herr Schmidbaur, the organist at
St Ulrich's, a fine old gentleman who's very well spoken;
and I then sight-read a sonata by Beecke that was quite
hard and *miserable al solito*; I can't begin to tell you how
the Kapellmeister and organist crossed themselves. Both
here and in Munich I've played my 6 sonatas many
times from memory. I played the fifth one in G at the
aristocrats' concert in the Bauernstube. The last one, in
D, sounds amazing on *Stein's* pianoforte. The device that
you depress with your knee is also better made on his
instrument than on others. I scarcely need to touch it and
it works; and as soon as you remove your knee even a
little, you no longer hear the slightest reverberation.
Tomorrow I may get round to his organs – – I mean, *to
write about them*; I'm saving up his little daughter till the
end. When I told Herr *Stein* that I'd like to play on his
organ as the organ was my passion, he was very surprised
and said: What, a man like you, so great a keyboard player
wants to play on an instrument that has no douceur,
no expression, no piano or forte but always sounds the
same? – – None of that matters. In my eyes and ears
the organ is the king of instruments. Well, as you like.
We went off together. I could already tell from what he

said that he didn't think I'd do much on his organ and that – for example – I'd play in a way more suited to a piano. He told me that Schubart had asked to be shown his organ, and I was afraid – he said – as Schubart had told everyone, and the church was quite full; for I thought he'd be all spirit, fire and speed, none of which works on the organ; but as soon as he started I changed my mind. I said only this: What do you think, Herr Stein? Do you think I'll run all over the organ? – – Oh, you, that's quite different. We reached the choir. I began to improvise, by which point he was already laughing, and then a fugue. I can well believe – he said – that you enjoy playing the organ if you play like that – – at first the pedal was a little strange as it wasn't divided. It began with C, then D, E in the same row. But with us D and E are above, as E flat and F sharp are here. But I soon got used to it. I also played on the old organ at St Ulrich's. The steps up to it are a nightmare. I asked if someone could play on it for me as I wanted to go down and listen. From up there the organ is totally ineffectual. But I could make nothing of it, as the young choirmaster, a priest, played only scales, so it was impossible to form any impression. And when he tried to play some chords, he produced only discords as it was out of tune. After that we had to go to a coffee-room as my mother and cousin and Herr Stein were with us. A certain Pater Aemilian, an arrogant ass and a simpleton of his profession, was in an especially hearty mood. He kept wanting to joke with my cousin, but she just made fun of him − − finally, when he was drunk (which didn't take long), he started to talk about music. He sang a canon and I said I'd never in my whole life heard a finer one. I said I'm sorry, I can't join in as I've no natural gift for intoning. That doesn't matter, he said. He started. I was the third voice, but I made up some very different words, for example, O you prick, lick my arse. *Sotto voce* to my cousin. We laughed about it for half an hour. He said to me: if only we could have spent longer together. I'd like to discuss the art of composition with you. Then the discussion would soon be over, I said. *Get lost*. To be continued.

W. A. Mozart

Leopold Mozart to his son, 23 October 1777, Salzburg

Mon très cher Fils,

I must congratulate you on your name day! But what can I wish you today that I don't always wish you? – – I wish you the grace of God, that it may accompany you everywhere and never abandon you, as indeed it will never do if you strive to fulfil the obligations of a true Catholic Christian.

You know me. – I'm no pedant, I'm not holier than thou, and I'm certainly no hypocrite: but you surely won't refuse a request from your father? – It is this: that you should be concerned for your soul's welfare and not cause your father any anxiety in his hour of death, so that at that difficult time he won't have to reproach himself for neglecting your soul's salvation. Farewell! Be happy! Lead a sensible life! Honour and esteem your mother, who has much toil in her old age, love me as I love you. Your truly solicitous father

Leop. Mozart

Leopold Mozart to his son,
24 November 1777, Salzburg

Mon très cher Fils,

I really don't know what to say, I was so stunned by your last letter of the 16th. In it you announced with a display of the *greatest nonchalance* that Herr *Schmalz* – presumably the father, brother or relation of Herr Schmalz of the leather factory in Munich or possibly even Herr Schmalz himself – had apologized for the fact that he had no instructions to give you any money. I can well believe that; and he was right: you should have asked Herr Herzog or the firm of Nocker & Schiedl to provide you with a little extra credit, *as I used to do*: for they had no orders from Hagenauer's house to extend this credit elsewhere, and no businessman exceeds his literal orders: but it would have been done if you'd asked them. But this incident was described in such matter-of-fact and indifferent terms as though I'd whole chests full of money and should have been terribly annoyed that you'd not been paid at once. I won't waste time with a long-winded account of our circumstances, you know them yourself, as does Mama, and in my letter *of the 20th* I listed the main items, although I forgot a sizeable *sum* that we owe to Hagenauer *for goods* but with whom we're not *writing up a single farthing more on credit*. But what amazed me most of all on receiving your letter was that you suddenly came out with this story without telling me about it in your previous letter, in which you simply said that money would have been more useful and appropriate for your journey than a trinket, as you knew even then that you were low on funds. If Herr Schmalz had been willing, I would have been lumbered with instructions for payment *without having received the slightest advance notice* and at a time *when I suspected nothing*. That's a pretty state of affairs indeed! – I leave you to think it over, in the light of my present circumstances. You wrote to me from Augsb. that you'd lost only 27 florins. – According to my own calculations, you must still have 170 florins even if you'd lost 30 florins. Even if that stupid trip to Mannheim via Wallerstein cost you 70 florins, you should still be left with 100 florins. Even if it cost you more, *can you really not have enough left* to be able to make the journey to Mainz? You'd then be near Frankfurt and if absolutely necessary would be able to draw a little with your second letter of credit from Herr Bolongaro in Frankfurt. Then you'd only have to ask some businessman in Mainz who's in contact with Herr Bolongaro; he would have undertaken to send the letter of credit to Herr Bolong. and to draw what you require.

Wouldn't this have been more sensible than to settle

down in Mannheim and squander your money to no avail, as this money would presumably have enabled you to make the journey, which would have cost perhaps 15 or 16 florins. It's only $1\frac{1}{4}$ stages to *Worms*, 2 to Oppenheim and 1 to Mainz, so only $3\frac{3}{4}$ in all. And even if you'd had little or no money on your arrival, we have acquaintances there who would help you, and no gentleman need be ashamed if he hasn't a farthing in his pocket but can produce a letter of credit: this can happen to the wealthiest and most distinguished people, indeed it's a maxim when travelling that, if possible, you should carry only as much money as you need. I'm still in the dark and if I speak of *Mainz* it's pure supposition as you haven't done me the honour in any of your letters of telling me where you are intending to go, only at the very last moment did you write to me from Augsb. and say you were going to Wallerstein; and Herr Stein wrote to say that you left for Wallerstein and Mannheim at half past 7 on Sunday. But such things should be announced some time in advance, as I can sometimes make useful preparations and send reminders, just as I was at pains to do by writing to Herr Otto and Herr Pfeil in Frankfurt. – – Of course, your journey is no concern of mine! Isn't that so? – – You could, of course, have taken a very different route from Mannheim: namely, Würzburg and from there to the Margrave of Darmstadt, then Frankfurt and Mainz. But how can I guess what you're thinking or make suggestions as I'm never consulted and didn't know how things stood in Mannheim, indeed to judge by your letter in which you had an opportunity to speak so familiarly with the elector I was bound to assume that you had very different plans and were intending to stay there for some time; all of which – whatever your opinions, inclinations, aims etc. may be – you should have reported honestly and in good time as it takes *12 days* to receive and reply to a letter even if all goes smoothly. But you didn't bother to consider this either as in your last letter of the 16th you wrote that *I could continue to write to you in Mannheim*, although it would be 12 days at the quickest before you received this letter, in other words, not until the 28th, by which time Herr Herzog will long since have replied and you will have left. But I did not receive your letter until Friday the 21st, as a present on our *wedding day*, and was unable therefore to reply until the 24th; you'll have read this letter – God knows where – on 1 or 2 December. Neither of you must think that I don't know how many incidental expenses are incurred on a journey and how money vanishes into thin air, especially when one's overgenerous or too kind. My dear wife prided herself on getting up early, on not lingering and on doing everything quickly and economically. *16 days in Munich*, *14 days in Augsburg* and now, according to your letter of *16 Nov.*, *17 days in Mannheim*, which, including the time spent waiting for a reply from Augsb., will turn out to be 3 weeks. That's sorcery indeed; you've been away 8 weeks, in other words, 2 months, and you're already in Mannheim? – – That's incredibly quick! When we travelled to England, we spent *9 days* in Munich, called on the *elector* and Duke *Clemens*, and had to wait for our present. – We were *15 days* in Augsb., but we gave *3 concerts* there, namely, on 28 and 30 June and 4 July. – We left Salzburg on *9 June* and did not arrive in Munich until the 12th as new wheels had to be made in Wasserburg, yet in spite of this we were in Schwetzingen by *13 July*, although we broke our journey in Ulm, Ludwigsburg and Bruchsal. So you see that your long and unnecessary stay has ruined everything, the most beautiful autumn in living memory has come and gone, and so far you've regarded your journey as no more than a pleasure trip and spent the time enjoying yourselves: now the bad weather, shorter days and cold are here, with more of the same to come, while your prospects and goals are now correspondingly expensive and distant.

You can't spend the whole winter travelling; and if you plan to stay anywhere, it should be in a large town with lots of people where there are hopes and opportunities of earning some money: and where is such a place to be found in the whole of this region? – Apart from Paris: – – but life in Paris requires a completely different attitude to life, a different way of thinking, you have to be attentive and every day think of ways of earning money and exercise extreme politeness in order to ingratiate yourself with people of standing: I'll write more on this in my next letter, in which I shall also set out my ideas on a quite different route that may be worth taking and which, I believe, will get you to Paris more quickly, namely, from *Koblenz* to *Trier, Luxembourg, Sedan*, where Herr *Ziegenhagen*, who visited us with Herr Wahler, has a textile factory. Perhaps he'll be there now. Then Rethel, *Rheims*, Soissons and Paris. Note that from Paris to Rethel there are 22 French post stages. From Rethel it's only a stone's throw to Sedan – Luxembourg, too, isn't far, and Trier is close to Luxembourg. Luxembourg is an imposing fortress and there'll be lots of officers there. *Rheims* and *Soissons* are large towns. In all these places it will be relatively easy to earn some money in order to recover your travelling expenses as virtuosos rarely visit such places. By contrast, it's 34 post stages from Brussels to Paris, and these cost us *20 louis d'or* for 6 horses, without our receiving a farthing in return. And between Koblenz and Brussels there's nothing that can be done, except perhaps with the elector of Cologne. Perhaps? – And what about Brussels? – – – – –

Meanwhile, whichever route you take, make sure that you obtain some letters of recommendation to take with you to Paris, it doesn't matter who writes them – businessmen, courtiers etc. etc. And is there no French ambassador or resident in Mainz or Koblenz? I don't think there is. You haven't got any letters of recommendation, whereas I had a lot; they're vital in providing you with both patronage and contacts. A journey like this is no joke, you've no experience of this sort of thing, you need to have other, more important thoughts on your mind than foolish games, you have to try to anticipate a hundred different things, otherwise you'll suddenly find yourself in the shit without any money, – – and where you've no money you'll have no friends either, even if you give a hundred lessons for nothing, and even if you write sonatas and spend every night fooling around from 10 till 12 instead of devoting yourself to more important matters. Then try asking for credit! – That'll wipe the smile off your face. I'm not blaming you for a moment for placing the Cannabichs under an obligation to you by your acts of kindness, that was well done: but you should have devoted a few of your otherwise idle hours each evening to your father, who is so concerned about you, and sent him not simply a mishmash tossed off in a hurry but a proper, confidential and detailed account of the expenses incurred on your journey, of the money you still have left, of the journey you plan to take in future and of your intentions in Mannheim etc. etc. In short, you should have sought my advice; I hope you'll be sensible enough to see this, for who has to shoulder this whole burden if not your poor old father? As I've already said, I didn't receive your letter until the 21st and was unable to reply until today. Yesterday, the 23rd, I confessed my sins at Holy Trinity and with tears in my eyes commended you both to the protection of Almighty God. In the afternoon we had target practice. The prize was offered by Cajetan Antretter and I won. *Herr Bullinger*, who sends his best wishes, was also somewhat taken aback by your letter and it struck me that, in the present serious situation, he didn't appreciate your joke about a public debt. At half past 5 I then went to see Herr Hagenauer to ask him *that if Messrs Nocker & Schiedl had not informed him by post that they had transferred some money to you, he might care to write to Augsb. by today's post.* I returned to the shop this morning and spoke to Herr Joseph. I discovered that although they'd received letters from *Nocker & Schiedl,* there'd been no word about you. He promised to write today. I've now done all I can and hope that in the meantime you'll have received some money, *Nocker* & Schiedl won't send me a report until they know how much you've been given. NB: It's always better when drawing money to accept not *florins* but the local currency, e.g., 6, 7 etc. *louis d'or, carolins* or whatever. I've now told you what was weighing on my mind, it is God's own truth. You'll have to learn for yourself that it is no joke to undertake a journey like this and to have to live on random income: above all you must pray most earnestly to God for good health, be on your guard against wicked people, earn money by every means that is known and available to you, and then spend it with the greatest care. I prefer to give too little to someone who is travelling with me and whom I may never see again and risk being called a skinflint, rather than have him laugh at me behind my back for giving him too much. I've no more paper, and I'm tired, especially my eyes.

Nannerl and I wish you the best of health and with all

our hearts kiss you a million times. I am your old husband and father but NB not your son

Mozart

I hope you'll have received my letter of the 20th in which I told you to write to *Monsieur Grimm* in Paris, also what you should write to the Prince of Chiemsee in Munich. By the next post I'll send you a list of all the stages to Paris and my opinion etc., also a list of all our former acquaintances in Paris. *Addio*.

Mozart to his father,
29 November 1777, Mannheim

Mon très cher Père,

I received your letter of the 24th this morning and see from it that you're unable to reconcile yourself to fate, be it good or bad, when it takes us by surprise; until now, and as things stand, the four of us have never been happy or unhappy, and for that I thank God. You reproach us both for many things, without our deserving it. We are not incurring any expenses that are not necessary; and what is necessary when travelling you know as well as we do, if not better. That we stayed so long in Munich was the fault of no one but *myself*; and if I'd been alone, I'd certainly have stayed in Munich. Why did we spend 2 weeks in Augsburg? – – I'm tempted to think that you didn't receive my letters from Augsburg. – – I wanted to give a concert – I was let down; meanwhile a whole week went by. I was absolutely determined to leave. They wouldn't let me. They wanted me to give a concert; I wanted them to beg me. And so they did. I gave a concert. There are your 2 weeks. Why did we go straight to Mann-heim? – – I answered this question in my last letter. Why are we still here? – – Yes – – can you really think that I'd remain somewhere for no reason? – – But I could have told my father – – all right, you shall know the reason and indeed the whole course of events. But God knows that I had no wish to speak about it because I was unable to go into detail – any more than I can today – and I know you well enough to appreciate that a *vague* account would have caused you worry and distress, something I've always tried to avoid; but if you ascribe the cause to my negligence, thoughtlessness and indolence, I can only thank you for your high opinion of me and sincerely regret that you don't know your own son.

I'm not thoughtless but am prepared for anything and as a result can wait patiently for whatever the future holds in store, and I'll be able to endure it—as long as my hon-our and the good name of Mozart don't suffer in consequence. Well, if it must be so, then let it be so. But I must ask you at the outset not to rejoice or grieve pre-maturely; for whatever happens, all is well as long as we remain healthy; for happiness consists simply in our imagination. Last Tuesday week, the 18th, the day before St Elisabeth's Day, I saw Count Savioli in the morning and asked him if there was any chance that the elector would keep me here this winter? – – I wanted to teach the young princes. He said yes, I'll suggest it to the elector; and if it's up to me, it will certainly happen. That after-noon I saw Cannabich and as it was at his suggestion that I'd been to see the count, he asked me at once if I'd been there. – I told him all that had happened, he said to me I'd very much like you to spend the winter here with us, but I'd like it even more if you had a proper, permanent appointment. I said that there was nothing I'd like more than to be always near them but that I really didn't know how it would be possible for me to stay permanently. You've already got two Kapellmeisters, so I don't know what I could do, as I wouldn't like to be under *Vogler*! Nor shall you, he said. None of the members of the orchestra here is under the Kapellmeister or even under the intendant. The elector could make you his chamber composer. Wait, I'll speak to the count about it. There was a big concert on Thursday. When the count saw me, he apologized for not having said anything, but the galas were still going on; but as soon as the galas were over, namely, on Monday, he would certainly speak to the elector. I left it for 3 days, and as I'd heard nothing, I went to see him in order to make enquiries. He said: My dear Monsieur Mozart (this was Friday, namely, yesterday), there was a hunt today so I've been unable to *ask* the elector; but by this time tomorrow I shall certainly be able to give you an answer: I begged him not to forget. To tell the truth, I was rather angry when I left him and decided to take the young count my six easiest variations on Fischer's minuet – which I'd already had copied out here for this very purpose – in order to have an opportunity to speak to the elector in person. When I arrived, you can't imagine how pleased the governess was to see

me. I received a most courteous welcome. When I took
out the variations and said that they were for the count,
she said Oh, that's good of you; but have you also got
something for the countess? – – Not yet, I said, but if I
were to stay here long enough to write something, I'll – –
By the way, she said, I'm glad that you'll be staying here
all winter. Me? – – I didn't know that! – – That surprises
me. It's curious. The elector himself told me so recently.
By the way, he said, Mozart is staying here this winter.
Well, if he did indeed say that, then he's the one person
who *can* say it, for without the elector I certainly can't
remain here. I told her the whole story. We agreed that
I'd return the next day – namely, *today* – after 4 o'clock
and bring something for the countess. You'll speak to the
elector – before I arrive – and he'll still be with you when
I get there. I went back there today, but he didn't come.
But I'll go again tomorrow. I've written a rondeau for the
countess. Don't I have reason enough to remain here and
await the outcome? – – Should I leave now that the greatest step has been taken? –   I now have a chance to speak
to the elector himself. I think I shall probably remain here
all winter as the elector is fond of me, he thinks highly of
me and knows what I can do. I hope to be able to give
you some good news in my next letter. I beg you once
again not to rejoice or worry too soon and to confide this
story in no one except Herr Bullinger and my sister. I'm
sending my sister the allegro and andante from the sonata
for Mlle Cannabich. The rondeau will follow shortly. It

would have been too much to send them all together.
You'll have to make do with the original; you can have
it copied more easily at 6 kreuzers a page than I can
at 24 kreuzers. Don't you find that expensive? – – Adieu.
I kiss your hands 100,000 times and embrace my sister
with all my heart. I am your obedient son

Wolfgang Amadé Mozart

You'll probably already have heard a little of the sonata,
as it's sung, banged out, fiddled and whistled at least
3 times a day at Cannabich's. – Only *sotto voce*, of course.

[*Maria Anna Mozart's postscript*]
My dear husband, I kiss you and Nannerl many 1000 times
and ask you to give our best wishes to all our acquaintances, I'll write more next time, but it's turned midnight,
addio, I remain your faithful wife

Maria Anna Mozart

Leopold Mozart to his wife and son,
4 December 1777, Salzburg

My Dear Wife and Dear Son,

I've no objection to your having to wait for what you told me about in your last letter, and there's nothing more that can be said about all that has happened on your journey and that has turned out differently from what I'd expected and worked out to our disadvantage and even caused us obvious harm, as it is all over and done with and can no longer be changed. – But the fact that you, my son, write *that all speculation is superfluous and of no avail as we cannot know what is to happen* – this is indeed ill considered and was undoubtedly written unthinkingly. No sensible person – I shall not say no Christian will deny that *everything will and must happen according to God's will*. But does it follow from this that we should act blindly, live carefree lives, make no provisions for the future and simply wait for things to befall us of their own accord? – Does God himself and, indeed, do all rational people not demand that in all our actions we consider their consequences and outcome, at least as far as our human powers of reason enable us to, and that we make every effort to see as far ahead as we can? – – If this is necessary in all our actions, how much more so is it in the present circumstances, on a journey? Or have you not already suffered the consequences of this? – – Is it enough for you to have taken the step *with the elector in order to remain there throughout the winter*? – – Should you not – shouldn't you long ago have thought of a plan that can be implemented if things don't work out: and shouldn't you have told me about it long ago and learnt my views on it? – – And now you write – what? If we were after all to leave here we'll go straight to Weilburg to the Princess of Nassau-Weilburg – for whom you wrote the sonatas in Holland – etc. – There we'll stay as long as *the officers' table* is to our liking – what sort of a tale is that? Like everything else you wrote, this is the language of a *desperate man* who is trying to console both himself and me. – – But there's still a *hope* that you'll receive 6 louis d'or, and that will make everything all right. – But my question to you now is whether you're certain that the princess is there: she won't be there without good reason as her husband is based in The Hague on account of his military office. Shouldn't you have told me about this long ago? – Another question: wouldn't you do better to go to Mainz – and from there to Weilburg via Frankfurt? After all, if you go from Mannheim to Weilburg, you'll cross the Frankfurt road: and as you're not staying in Weilburg for ever, the Mainz road will take you back through Frankfurt. If you first go to Mainz and then to Weilburg, you'll have only a short distance from Weilburg to Koblenz, which will presumably take you via *Nassau*. Or do you intend to avoid Mainz, where we've so many good friends and where we earned *200 florins from 3 concerts*, even without playing for the elector, who was ill. Tell me, my dear son, are these useless speculations? – – Your dear good Mama told me she'd keep a careful note of your expenses. Good! I've never asked for a detailed account and never thought of demanding one: but when you arrived in Augsburg you should have written to say: We paid such and such at Albert's in Munich, and such and such was spent on travelling expenses, so that we still have *such and such* a sum. From Augsb. you wrote to say that after taking account of the concert receipts you were about 20 florins out of pocket. In your 2nd letter from Mannheim you should at least have said that the journey cost us such and such an amount and we're *now* left with – –, so that I could have made arrangements in good time – – was my arrangement to send you a letter of credit in Augsburg a useless speculation? – – Do you really think that Herr Herzog – *who's a good old friend of mine* – would have provided you with money in response to all your letters from Mannheim if you'd not already given him a letter of credit? – – Certainly not! The most that he would have done would have been to make enquiries with me first. – – Why did I have to discover that you needed money only when you were in trouble? *You wanted to wait to see what the elector gave you*. Isn't that so? Perhaps in order to spare me the worry – – but it would have caused me less worry if I'd been told everything honestly and in good time, as I know better than either of you how one must be prepared for all eventualities on such a journey in order not to be placed in some terrible predicament at the very moment when one least expects it. – At such times all your *friends* disappear! *One must be cheerful; one must enjoy oneself!* But one must also find time *to give serious thought to these matters*, and this must be your main concern when travelling and when not a single day should be allowed to pass to your disadvantage – – the days slip past – days which are in any case very short at present and which all cost money at an inn. Merciful heavens! You ask me not to speculate now that *I'm 450 florins in debt entirely thanks to you two*. – And you think that you may be able to put me in a good mood by telling me a hundred foolish jokes. I'm pleased that you're in good spirits: but instead of the good wishes set out in the form of the alphabet, I'd have felt happier if you'd told me the reasons for, and the circumstances of, your journey to *Weilburg* and what you planned to do afterwards and, most of all, if you'd listened to my opinion; and this could have been done before a post day, as you can't only just have hit on the idea, nor can you know independently that the princess is there, unless someone had already suggested the idea to you. In a word, it is no idle speculation when one has something in mind and formulates 2 or 3 plans and makes all the necessary arrangements in advance so that

24

if one plan doesn't work out, one can easily turn to another. Anyone who acts otherwise is an unintelligent or thoughtless person who, especially *in today's world*, will always be left behind, no matter how clever he is, and who will even be unhappy as he will always be duped by flatterers, false friends and those who envy him. My son, to find *one man in a 1000* who is your true friend for reasons other than self-interest *is one of the greatest wonders of this world*. Examine all who call themselves your friends or who make a show of friendship and you'll find the reason why this is so. If they're not motivated by self-interest on their own account, then they'll be acting in the interests of some other friend whom they need; or they are your friends so that by singling you out they can annoy some third party. If nothing comes of *Mannheim*, you still have your plan to go to *Mainz, Frankfurt, Weilburg, Koblenz* etc.; one should always look for places as close to each other as possible so that, if you can, the journeys should be kept short and you can soon get to a place where you'll find a source of income. If this letter doesn't reach you in *Mannheim* and you're already in *Weilburg*, I can't help you. But if you're still in Mannheim and have to leave, then Mama will see from the map that your best plan is to go to *Mainz* first, otherwise you'll either have to forgo Mainz or retrace your steps a little. In Weilburg you need to bear in mind that you'll not find a *Catholic church* there as everyone is *Lutheran* or *Calvinist*. So I'd prefer you *not to spend too long* there.

And who told you that you'd have to go through the forest of Spessart to get from *Würzburg to Mannheim* as the *Spessart* is near *Aschaffenburg*, between *Fulda and Frankfurt*? – – This is no doubt some other trick that Herr Beecke has played on you. *Aschaffenburg* and *Würzburg* are 10 miles apart. – It may be that one drives past the forest on the right-hand side for some hours as one approaches Mannheim. But there's nothing near Würzburg, whether you've been there or not.

NB: I've another observation to make about any journey that you may choose to make from *Weilburg* to *Koblenz*, namely, that the road is across country and will be safer than the one from *Mainz* to *Koblenz*, which is too near the Rhine. I now want to know all your other plans, *I'd never have suspected that my own dear wife wouldn't have given me the occasional accurate account of your travelling expense, as I've twice asked about Albert's bill and should also have been told about the bill from the landlord of the Lamb etc. etc.* But I'm not allowed to know about all your expenses. *And so I must ask Mama to write me a confidential letter on this point – I don't want a wordy explanation but would just like to see from the landlord's bill how people have been treating you and where all the money has gone.* We must now give serious thought to the ways and means of getting you out of the present situation, of travelling as economically as possible and of making sensible arrangements, but at all events you must let me know at once what may be to our detriment or advantage. *On no account* must you *sell* the chaise.

May God keep both you and me well. Nannerl and I kiss you many 100,000,000 times. I am your own husband and father

Mzt

Count Czernin has asked me to give you his best wishes. There was a rumour not only that the archbishop will be sending Haydn to Italy but that he had already wanted to send him to Bozen with Triendl. But Herr Triendl excused himself. I beg you, my dear Wolfg., consider everything and don't always write about things when they're already over and done with. Otherwise we'll all be unhappy.

Leopold Mozart to his son,
5 February 1778, Salzburg

My Dear Son,

   In all probability this will be the last letter that you can be certain of receiving from me in Mannheim, and so it is addressed to you alone. How hard it is for me to accept that you're moving even further away from me is something you may perhaps be able to imagine, but you cannot feel as acutely as I do the weight that lies on my mind. If you take the trouble to recall what I did with you two children during your tender youth, you'll not accuse me of timidity but, like everyone else, will concede that I am a man and have always had the courage to risk everything. But I did everything with the greatest caution and consideration that were humanly possible: – one can't prevent accidents, for God alone can foretell the future. Until now, of course, we've been neither happy nor unhappy, but, thanks be to God, we've trodden a middle course. We've tried everything to make you happy and, through you, to make ourselves happier and at least to place your destiny on a firmer footing; but fate was against us. As you know, our last step has left me in very deep waters, and you also know that I'm now around 700 florins *in debt* and don't know how I shall *support myself, your mother and your sister* on my *monthly income*, for as long as I live I cannot *hope to receive another farthing* from *the prince*. So it must be clear as day to you that the future fate of your old parents and of your sister, who undoubtedly loves you with all her heart, lies solely in your hands. Ever since you were born and, indeed, before that – in other words, ever since I was married – there is no doubt that I've had a difficult time *providing a livelihood* for a wife and 7 children, 2 servants and Mama's mother, all on a fixed monthly income of only a little more than 20 florins, and to *pay for* accouchements, deaths and illnesses, expenses which, if you think them over, will convince you not only that I have never spent a farthing on the least pleasure for myself, but that, without God's special mercy, I'd never have managed to *keep out of debt* in spite of all my hopes and bitter efforts: yet this is *the first time I've been in debt*. I gave up every hour of my life to you 2 in the hope of ensuring not only that in due course you'd both be able to count on being able to provide for yourselves but that I too would be able to enjoy a peaceful old age and be accountable to God for my children's education, with no more cares but being able to live solely for my soul's salvation and calmly awaiting my end. But God has willed and ordained that I must once again take on the *undoubtedly wearisome task* of giving lessons and of doing so, moreover, in a town where these strenuous

29

efforts are so badly paid that it is not possible every month *to earn enough to support oneself and one's family*. Yet one must be glad and talk oneself hoarse in order to *earn* at least *something*. Not only do I not distrust you, my dear Wolfgang, no, not in the very least, but I place all my trust and hope in your filial love: all depends on your good sense, which you certainly have – if only you will listen to it – and on fortunate circumstances. This latter cannot be coerced; but you will always consult your good sense – at least I hope so and beg of you to do so.

You're now entering a completely different world: and you mustn't think that it is simply prejudice that makes me see Paris as such a dangerous place, *au contraire* – from my own experience I've no reason at all to regard Paris as so very dangerous. But my situation then could not be more different from yours now. We stayed with an ambassador, and on the second occasion in a self-contained apartment; I was a man of mature years and you were children; I avoided all contact with others and in particular *preferred not to become over-familiar with people of our own profession*; remember that I did the same in Italy. I made the acquaintance and sought out the friendship only of people of a higher social class – and among these only mature people, not young lads, not even if they were of the foremost rank. I never invited anyone to visit me regularly in my rooms in order to be able to maintain my freedom, and I always considered it more sensible to visit others at my convenience. If I don't like a person or if I'm working or have business to attend to, I can then stay away. – Conversely, if people come to me and behave badly, I don't know how to get rid of them, and even a person who is otherwise not unwelcome may prevent me from getting on with some important work. You're a young man of 22; and so you don't have that earnestness of old age that could deter a young lad of whatever social class, be he an adventurer, joker or fraud and be he young or old, from seeking out your acquaintance and friendship and drawing you into his company and then gradually into his plans. One is drawn imperceptibly into this and cannot then escape. I shan't even mention women, for here one needs the greatest restraint and reason, as nature herself is our enemy, and the man who does not apply his whole reason and show the necessary restraint will later do so in vain in his attempt to escape from the labyrinth, *a misfortune that mostly ends only in death*. You yourself may perhaps already have learnt from your limited experience how blindly we may often be taken in by jests, flatteries and jokes that initially seem unimportant but at which reason, when she awakes later on, is ashamed; I don't want to reproach you. I know that you love me not just as your father but also as your staunchest and surest friend; and that you know and realize that our happiness and misfortune and, indeed, my very life – whether I live to a ripe old age or die suddenly – are in your hands as much as God's. If I know you, I can hope for nothing but contentment, and this alone must console me during your absence, when I am deprived of a father's delight in hearing, seeing and embracing you. Live like a good Catholic, live and fear God, pray most fervently to Him in reverence and trust, and lead so Christian a life that, even if I am never to see you again, the hour of my death may be free from care. With all my heart I give you a father's blessing and remain until death your faithful father and surest friend

Leopold Mozart

Here are our Paris acquaintances, all of whom will be delighted to see you. [. . .]

[*Leopold's postscript to his wife on the envelope*]
My Dear Wife,

As you'll receive this letter on the 11th or 12th and as I doubt whether a further letter will reach Wolfg. in Mannheim, I'll take my leave of him with this enclosure! I'm writing this with tears in my eyes. Nannerl kisses her dear brother Wolfg. a million times. She would have added a note to my letter and said goodbye, but the letter was already full and in any case I didn't let her read it. We ask Wolfg. *to take care of his health and to stick to the diet that he got used to at home*; otherwise he'll have *to be bled* as soon as he arrives in Paris, *everything spicy* is bad for him. I

expect he'll take with him the big *Latin prayer book* that
contains *all the psalms* for the full office of Our Lady. If
he wants to have the *German* text of the office of Our Lady
in Mannheim in order to have it in German too, he'll have
to try to obtain the very smallest format as the Latin
psalms are difficult to understand. It would be better if
he also had them in German. Learned contrapuntal set-
tings of the psalms are also performed at the Concert
Spirituel; it's possible to gain a great reputation in this
way. Perhaps he could also have his *Misericordias* performed there. The opera singers aren't coming but have
gone instead to Straubing to entertain the Austrian officers. The prince has again forced the magistrature to hold
9 balls, the first one was yesterday and was attended by
30 persons; it lasted till half past one, but not a soul had
arrived by half past 9 and it wasn't till 10 that they started
dancing; 1 capon and 6 mugs of wine were consumed. I
hope you received the 2 sonatas for 4 hands, the Fischer
variations and the rondo, which were all parcelled up in
the same letter. – – The late Herr Adlgasser hasn't found
a decent bellows blower in the afterlife; the cathedral's
old bellows blower, the 80-year-old Thomas, has followed
him into the next world. The main news is that Mme
Barisani has become incredibly jealous of her old and
respectable husband as he and Checco have on a handful
of occasions been to perform at the home of handsome
Herr Freysauff, who has a relatively pretty but witless

wife. There was an incredible fuss. Farewell. We kiss you millions of times

Mzt

Everyone sends their best wishes, especially Herr Bull-inger and the wife of the sergeant of the bodyguards, Herr *Clessin*, Waberl Mölk etc.

Mozart to his father, 3 July 1778, Paris

Monsieur
mon très cher Père!

I have some very disagreeable and sad news for you, which is also the reason why I have been unable until now to reply to your last letter of the 11th. –

My dear mother is very ill – she was bled, as usual, and very necessary it was, too; she felt very well afterwards – but a few days later she complained of shivering and feverishness – she had diarrhoea and a headache – at first we just used our home remedies, antispasmodic powder, we'd like to have used the black one too, but we didn't have any and couldn't get any here, it's not known here even under the name of *Pulvis epilepticus*. – But when things started to get worse – she could hardly speak and lost her hearing so we had to shout – Baron *Grimm* sent his doctor – she's very weak and is still feverish and delirious – I'm told to be hopeful, but I'm not – for long days and nights I've been hovering between fear and hope – but I've resigned myself to God's will – and I hope that you and my dear sister will do the same; what other means is there to remain calm? – or, rather, calmer, as we can't be entirely calm; – come what may, I feel comforted – because I know that God, who orders everything for the best, however contrary it may seem to us, wills it so; for I believe – and I won't be persuaded otherwise – that no doctor, no individual, no misfortune and no accident can give a man his life or take it away, God alone can do that – these are only the instruments that He generally uses, although not always – after all, we can see people fainting, collapsing and dying – once our time comes, all remedies are useless, they hasten death rather than prevent it – we saw this in the case of our late friend Herr Heffner! – I'm not saying by this that my mother will and must die and that all hope is lost – she may yet be hale and hearty again, but only if God so wills it – after praying to my God with all my strength for health and life for my dear mother, I like to think this and derive comfort from such thoughts, as I then feel heartened, calmer and consoled – and you'll easily imagine that I need this! – Now for something different; let's banish these sad thoughts. Let us hope, but not too much; let us put our trust in God and console ourselves with the thought that all is well if it accords with the will of the Almighty as He knows best what is most advantageous and beneficial to our temporal and eternal happiness and salvation –

I've had to write a symphony to open the Concert Spirituel. It was performed to general acclaim on Corpus

Christi; I also hear that there was a report on it in the *Courrier de l'Europe*. – Without exception, people liked it. I was very afraid at the rehearsal as I've never in all my life heard anything worse; you can't imagine how twice in succession they bungled and scraped their way through it. – I was really very afraid – I'd have liked to rehearse it again, but there are always so many things to rehearse and so there was no more time; and so I had to go to bed with a fearful heart and in a discontented and angry frame of mind. The next day I decided not to go to the concert at all; but in the evening the weather was fine and so I decided to go, determined that if it went as badly as it had done during the rehearsal, I'd go into the orchestra, take the fiddle from the hands of the first violin, Herr Lahoussaye, and conduct myself. I prayed to *God* that it would go well because everything is to His greater glory and honour; and behold, the symphony started, Raaff was standing next to me, and in the middle of the opening allegro there was a passage that I knew very well people were bound to like, the whole audience was carried away by it – and there was loud applause – but as I knew when I wrote it what effect it would produce, I introduced it again at the end – now people wanted to have it encored. They liked the andante, too, but especially the final allegro – I'd heard that all the final allegros and opening ones too begin here with all the instruments playing together and generally in unison, and so I began mine with 2 violins only, playing piano for 8 whole bars, followed at once by a forte – the audience, as I expected, went 'shush' at the piano – then came the forte – and as soon as they heard it, they started to clap – I was so happy that as soon as the symphony was over I went to the Palais Royal – had a large ice – said the rosary, as I'd promised – and went home – just as I'm always happiest at home and always will be – or with some good, true, honest German who, if he's single, lives on his own as a good Christian or, if married, loves his wife and brings up his children well –

You probably already know that that godless arch-rogue Voltaire has died like a dog, like a beast – that's his reward! – As you say, we owe Tresel her wages for 5 quarters – you'll have realized long ago that I don't like it here – there are many reasons for this, but as I'm here, it would serve no useful purpose to go into them. It's not my fault and never will be, I'll do my very best – well, God will make all things right! – I've something in mind for which I pray to God every day – if it's His divine will, it will happen, if not, then I'm also content – at least I'll have done my part – when all is sorted out and if things work out as I want, you too must do your part or the whole business will be incomplete – I trust in your kindness to do so – but for the present you mustn't waste time thinking about it, the only favour I wanted to beg of you now is not to ask me to reveal my thoughts until it's time to do so.

As for the opera, it's now like this. It's very difficult to find a good libretto. The old ones are the best but they're not suited to the modern style, and the new ones are all useless; poetry was the one thing of which the French could be proud but this is now getting worse by the day – and yet poetry is the one thing that must be good here as they don't understand music – there are now 2 aria-based operas that I could write, one *en deux actes*, the other *en trois*. The one *en deux* is *Alexandre et Roxane* – but the poet who's writing it is still out of town – the one *en trois* is a translation of *Demofoonte* by Metastasio, combined with choruses and dances and in general arranged for the French theatre. Of this I've not yet been able to see anything –

Let me know if you've got Schroeter's concertos in Salzburg. And Hüllmandel's sonatas. – I was thinking of buying them and sending them to you. Both sets of pieces are very fine – I never thought of going to Versailles – I asked Baron Grimm and some other good friends for their advice – they all thought like me.

It's not much money, you have to spend 6 months languishing in a place where you can't earn anything else and your talent lies buried. Anyone in the king's service is forgotten in Paris. And then, to be an organist! – I'd like a decent appointment, but only as a Kapellmeister, and well paid.

Farewell for now – take care of your health, put your trust in God – it's there that you must find consolation; my dear mother is in the hands of the Almighty – if He returns her to us, as I hope, we shall thank Him for this mercy, but if it is His will to take her to Him, our fears and cares and despair will be of no avail – let us rather resign ourselves steadfastly to His divine will, fully convinced that it will be for our own good, for He does nothing without good cause – farewell, dearest Papa, keep well for my sake; I kiss your hands 1000 times and embrace my sister with all my heart. I am your most obedient son

Wolfgang Amadè Mozart

Mozart to his father, 9 July 1778, Paris

Monsieur
mon très cher Père!

  I hope that you are prepared to hear with fortitude a piece of news that could not be sadder or more painful – my last letter of the 3rd will have placed you in the position of knowing that the news, when it came, would not be good – that same day, the 3rd, at 10.21 in the evening, my mother passed away peacefully; – when I wrote to you, she was already enjoying the delights of heaven – by then it was all over – I wrote to you during the night – I hope that you and my dear sister will forgive me this slight but very necessary deception – concluding from my own grief and sadness what yours must be, I couldn't possibly bring myself to spring such a terrible piece of news on you – but I hope that you're both now ready to hear the worst and that, after giving way to natural and only too justified grief and tears, you will eventually resign yourselves to God's will and worship His inscrutable, unfathomable and all-wise providence – you'll easily be able to imagine what I have had to bear – what courage and fortitude I needed

to endure it all calmly as things grew progressively worse –
and yet God in His goodness granted me this mercy – I
have suffered enough anguish and wept enough tears –
but what use was it all? – and so I had to console myself;
you, my dear father and sister, must do the same! – Weep,
weep your fill – but ultimately you must take comfort, –
remember that Almighty God willed it so – and what can
we do against Him? – We should rather pray and thank
Him that it all turned out for the best – for she died a very
happy death; – in these sad circumstances, I consoled
myself with three things, namely, my entire trust and submission in God's will – then the fact that I was present at
so easy and beautiful a death, as I imagined how happy
she had become in a single moment – how much happier
she is now than we are – so much so that at that moment
I wanted to take the same journey as she had just done – in
turn this wish and desire gave rise to my third source of
consolation, namely, that she is not lost to us for ever – we
shall see her again – we shall be happier and more contented to be with her than we have been in this world; we
do not know when our time may come – but this is no
cause for anxiety – when God wills it, then I too shall will
it – well, God's most hallowed will has been done – let us
therefore say a devout prayer for her soul and proceed to
other matters, there is a time for everything – I'm writing
this at the home of Madame d'Épinay and Monsieur
Grimm, where I'm now lodging, a pretty little room with
a very pleasant view and, so far as my state allows, I'm

happy here – it will help me to regain my contentment to hear that my dear father and sister have accepted God's will with composure and fortitude and that they trust in Him with all their hearts in the firm conviction that He orders all things for the best – dearest father! Look after yourself! – Dearest sister – look after yourself – you've not yet enjoyed your brother's kind heart as he's not yet been able to demonstrate it – dearest father and sister – look after your health – remember that you have a son and a brother who is doing everything in his power to make you happy – knowing full well that one day you'll not refuse to grant him his desire and his happiness – which certainly does him honour – and that you'll do everything possible to make him happy – Oh, then we'll live together as peacefully, honourably and contentedly as is possible in this world – and finally, when God wills it, we shall meet again there – for this we are destined and created –

Your last letter of 29 June has arrived safely and I'm pleased to learn that you are both well, all praise and thanks be to God, I couldn't help laughing at your account of Haydn's drunkenness, – if I'd been there, I'd certainly have whispered in his ear: *Adlgasser*. But it's a disgrace that such an able man should be rendered incapable of performing his duties and have only himself to blame for it – in a post that's in God's honour – when the archbishop and the whole court are there – and the whole church is full of people – it's appalling – this is

also one of the main reasons why I detest Salzburg – the
coarse, ill-mannered and dissolute court musicians – no
honest man of good breeding could live with them; –
instead of taking an interest in them, he should be
ashamed of them! – also – and this is probably the
reason – the musicians aren't very popular with us and
are simply not respected – if only the orchestra were
organized as it is in Mannheim! – the discipline that
obtains in that orchestra! – the authority that Cannabich
wields – there everything is taken seriously; Cannabich,
who's the best music director I've ever seen, is loved and
feared by his subordinates. – He's also respected by the
whole town, as are his troops – but they certainly behave
very differently – they're well-mannered, dress well, don't
frequent taverns and don't get drunk – but this can never
be the case with you, unless, that is, the prince trusts you
or me and gives us full authority, *at least as far as the orchestra is concerned* – otherwise it's no good; in *Salzburg*
everyone – or rather no one – bothers about the
orchestra – if I were to take it on, I'd have to have a completely free hand – the chief steward should have nothing
to say to me on orchestral matters and, indeed, on anything bound up with the orchestra. A courtier can't stand
in for a Kapellmeister, though a Kapellmeister could no
doubt stand in for a courtier – by the way, the elector is
now back in Mannheim – Madame Cannabich and her
husband are in correspondence with me. I'm afraid that
the orchestra will be much reduced in size, which would

be an eternal shame, but if this doesn't happen, I may still remain hopeful – you know that there's nothing I want more than a good position, good in character and good in terms of the money – it doesn't matter where it is – as long as it's in a Catholic area. – You acted in a masterly way, just like Ulysses, throughout the whole affair with Count Starhemberg – only continue as before and don't allow yourself to be taken in – and in particular you should be on your guard if conversation turns to that arrogant goose – I know her, and you can be assured that she has sugar and honey on her lips but pepper in her head and heart – it's entirely natural that the whole business is still open to discussion and that many points must be conceded before I could make up my mind and that even if everything were all right I'd still prefer to be anywhere else but Salzburg – but I don't need to worry, as it's unlikely that everything will be granted to me as I'm asking for so much –. But it's not impossible – I'd not hesitate for a moment if everything were properly organized – if only to have the pleasure of being with you – but if the Salzburgers want me, they must satisfy me and all my wishes – otherwise they'll certainly not get me. – So the abbot of Baumberg has died the usual abbot's death! – I didn't know that the abbot of the Holy Cross had died too – I'm very sorry – he was a good, honest, decent man; so you didn't think that Dean Zöschinger would be made abbot? – Upon my honour, I never imagined it otherwise; I really don't know who else it could have been! – Of course, he's a good abbot for the orchestra! – So the *young lady's* daily walk with her faithful lackey bore fruit after all! – They were certainly busy and haven't been idle – the devil makes work for idle hands: – so the amateur theatricals have finally started up? – But how long will they last? – I don't suppose Countess Lodron will be wanting any more concerts like the last one – Czernin is a young whippersnapper and Brunetti a foul-mouthed oaf.

My friend Raaff is leaving tomorrow; but he's going via Brussels to Aix-la-Chapelle and Spa – and from there to Mannheim; he'll let me know as soon as he gets there, for we intend to stay in touch – he sends you and my sister his good wishes, even though he doesn't know you. You say in your letter that you've heard no more about my composition pupil for a long time – that's true, but what shall I tell you about her? – She's not the sort of person who will ever become a composer – all my efforts are in vain – in the first place, she's thoroughly stupid and also thoroughly lazy – I told you about the opera in my last letter – as for Noverre's ballet, all I've ever said is that he may write a new one – he needed just half a ballet and so I wrote the music for it – in other words, 6 numbers are by others and consist entirely of dreadful old French airs, whereas I've written the symphony and contredanses, making 12 pieces in all – the ballet has already been given 4 times to great acclaim – but I'm now absolutely determined not to write anything else unless

I know in advance what I'm going to get for it – I did this just as a favour for Noverre. – Monsieur Wendling left on the last day of May – if I wanted to see Baron Bagge, I'd have to have very good eyes as he's not here but in London – is it possible that I've not already told you this? – You'll see that in future I'll answer all your letters accurately – it's said that Baron Bagge will be returning soon, which I should like very much – for many reasons – but especially because there's always an opportunity at his house to hold proper rehearsals – Kapellmeister Bach will also be here soon – I think he'll be writing an opera – the French are asses and will always remain so, they can do nothing themselves – they have to rely on foreigners. I spoke to Piccinni at the Concert Spirituel – he's very polite to me and I to him – whenever we happen to meet – otherwise I've not made any new acquaintances – either with him or with other composers – I know what I'm doing – and so do they – and that's enough: – I've already told you that my symphony was a great success at the Concert Spirituel. If I'm asked to write an opera, it'll no doubt be a source of considerable annoyance, but I don't mind too much as I'm used to it – if only the confounded French language weren't such a dastardly enemy of music! – It's pitiful – German is divine in comparison. – And then there are the singers – – they simply don't deserve the name as they don't sing but scream and howl at the tops of their voices, a nasal, throaty sound – I'll have to write a French oratorio for

47

the Concert Spirituel next Lent – the director Legros is
amazingly taken with me; I should add that although I
used to see him every day, I've not seen him since Easter,
I was so annoyed that he'd not performed my sinfonia
concertante; I often visited his house in order to see Monsieur Raaff and each time had to pass his rooms – on each
occasion the servants and maids saw me and on each
occasion I asked them to give him my best wishes. – I
think it's a shame that he didn't perform it, people would
have liked it – but he no longer has any opportunity to
do so. Where could he find 4 such people for it? One day,
when I was planning to visit Raaff, he wasn't at home but
I was assured that he'd soon be back. And so I waited –
Monsieur Legros came into the room – it's a miracle that
I've finally had the pleasure of seeing you again – yes,
I've got so much to do – are you staying for lunch? – I'm
sorry, but I've a prior engagement. – Monsieur Mozart,
we must spend more time together; – it'll be a pleasure. –
Long silence – finally: by the way, won't you write a grand
symphony for me for Corpus Christi? – Why not? – But
can I rely on it? – Oh yes, as long as I can rely on its being
performed – and that it doesn't suffer the same fate as the
sinfonia concertante – then the dance began – he apologized as best he could – but there wasn't much he could
say – in a word, the symphony was universally liked – and
Legros is so pleased that he says it's his best symphony –
only the andante hasn't had the good fortune to win his
approval – he says it contains too many modulations and

that it's too long – but this is because the audience forgot
to clap as loudly and make as much noise as they did for
the first and final movements – but the andante won the
greatest approval *from me* and from all the connoisseurs
and music lovers and most other listeners – it's exactly
the opposite of what Legros says – it's entirely natural –
and short. – But in order to satisfy him – and, as he
claims, several others – I've written another one – each
is fitting in its own way – for each has a different
character – but I like the last one even more – when I
have a moment, I'll send you the symphony, together
with the violin tutor, some keyboard pieces and Vogler's
Tonwissenschaft und Tonsezkunst – and I shall then want to
know what you think about them – the symphony will
be performed for the second time – with the new
andante – on 15 August – the Feast of the Assumption –
the symphony is in re and the andante in sol – you're not
supposed to say D or G here. – Well, Legros is now right
behind me. – It's time to start thinking about ending this
letter – if you write to me, I think it would be better if
you were to do so *chez Monsieur Le Baron de Grimm, Chaus-
sée d'Antin près le Boulevard* – Monsieur Grimm will be
writing to you himself very shortly. He and Madame
d'Épinay both ask to be remembered to you and send
you their heartfelt condolences – but they hope that you
will be able to remain composed in the face of a matter
that can't be changed – take comfort – and pray fervently,
this is the only expedient that is left to us – I was going

to ask you to have Holy Masses said at Maria Plain and Loreto – I've also done so here. As for the letter of recommendation for Herr Beer, I don't think it'll be necessary to send it to me – I still haven't met him; I know only that he's a good clarinettist but a dissolute companion – I don't like associating with such people – it does one no credit; and I've no wish to give him a letter of recommendation – I'd be truly ashamed to do so – even if he could do something for me! – But he's by no means respected – many people haven't even heard of him – Of the 2 Stamitzes, only the younger one is here – the older (the real composer *à la* Hafeneder) is in London – they're 2 wretched scribblers – and gamblers – drunkards – and whoremongers – not the kind of people for me – the one who's here has scarcely a decent coat to his back – by the way, if things don't work out with Brunetti, I'd very much like to recommend a good friend of mine to the archbishop as first violin, a decent, honest, upstanding man – a stolid individual; – I'd put him at around 40 – a widower – he's called Rothfischer – he's concert master to the princess of Nassau-Weilburg at Kirchheimbolanden – between ourselves, he's dissatisfied as the prince doesn't like him – or rather he doesn't like *his music* – he's commended himself to me and it would give me real pleasure to help him – he's the best of men. – Adieu. I kiss your hands 100,000 times and embrace my sister with all my heart. I am your most obedient son

Wolfgang Amadè Mozart

Leopold Mozart to his wife and son, 13 July 1778, Salzburg

My Dear Wife and Son,

In order not to miss your name day, my dear wife, I'm writing to you today, even though the letter will no doubt arrive a few days early. I wish you a million joys in being able to celebrate it once more and ask Almighty God to keep you well on this day and for many years to come and allow you to live as contented a life as is possible in this inconstant world theatre. I'm absolutely convinced that for you to be truly happy you need your husband and daughter. God in His unfathomable decree and most holy providence will do what is best for us. Would you have thought a year ago that you'd be spending your next name day in Paris? − − However incredible this would have seemed to many people then, although not to ourselves, it is possible that with God's help we may be reunited even before we expect it: for my one concern is that I am separated from you and *living so far away, so very far away from you*; otherwise we're well, God be praised! We both kiss you and Wolfgang a million times and beg you above all to take great care of your health. − *The theatre of war has finally opened!* In Paris you'll already know that on the 5th of this month the king of Prussia entered Bohemia from Glatz and that he's passed through Nachod and penetrated as far as Königgrätz. War was bound to break out as neither power could withdraw its armies without losing face. For several weeks Austria, with its marches and countermarches, has provided the king with occasional opportunities to make an incursion and launch an attack: but the king didn't think it advisable to undertake such an attack; now the emperor has established a very powerful *false arsenal* at Nachod, and this persuaded the king to attack. But the arsenal was a *feint* and contained only a semblance of the real thing. They had to take this risk, whatever the outcome, as Austria was neither able nor willing to be the aggressor, while the Croats were merely an advance guard (the only position in which they can really be used) and could barely be restrained any longer, as these people always hope to win booty, which is why they're so keen to go to war. The Saxon troops have formed an alliance with Prussia, and it's presumably true that they've joined forces with Prince Heinrich and will no doubt attack *Eger* and the *Upper* Palatinate. More news will no doubt arrive with the next post: this came with the Austrian post on the 11th. This war will be one of the bloodiest, the king wants to die a glorious death, and the emperor wants to start his army life on an equally glorious note.

I wrote the foregoing yesterday, the 12th. This morning, the

13th, shortly before 10 o'clock, I received your distressing letter of 3 July. You can well imagine how we are both feeling. We wept so much that we could scarcely read your letter. – And your sister! – Great God in your mercy! May your most hallowed will be done! My dear son! For all that I am resigned as far as possible to God's will, you'll none the less find it entirely human and natural that I'm almost unable to write for weeping. What am I to conclude from all this –? Only that even as I write these lines, she is presumably already dead – or that she has recovered, for you wrote on the 3rd and today is already the 13th. You say that after being bled she felt well, but that a few days later she complained of shivering and feverishness. The last letter from the two of you was dated 12 June, and in it she wrote – *I was bled yesterday*: so that was the 11th – and why was it done on a Saturday – a fast day? – – I expect she ate some meat. She waited too long to be bled. Knowing her very well, I remember that she likes to put things off, especially in a foreign place, where she'd first have to enquire after a surgeon. Well, so the matter stands – it can't be helped any longer – I have complete confidence in your filial love and know that you have taken all possible care of your mother, who is undoubtedly *good*, and that if God restores her to us, you will always continue to do so – your *good* mother, who always saw you as *the apple of her eye* and whose love for you was exceptional, who was exceedingly proud of you and who – I know this better than you – lived for you alone.

But if all our hopes are in vain! Could we really have lost her! – Good God! *You need friends, honest friends!* Otherwise you'll lose everything, what with the funeral expenses etc. My God! There are many expenses about which you know nothing and where strangers are cheated – taken for a ride – tricked – put to unnecessary expense and exploited if they don't have honest friends: you can have no conception of this. If this misfortune has befallen you, ask Baron Grimm if you can store your mother's effects at his house, so that you don't have to keep an eye on so many things: or lock everything up, because if you're often away for whole days at a time, people could break into your room and rob you. God grant that all my precautions are unnecessary: but you will recognize your father in this. My dear wife! My dear son! – as she fell ill a few days after being bled, she must have been ill since 16 or 17 June. But you waited too long – she thought she'd get better through bed rest – by dieting – by her own devices, I know how it is, one hopes for the best and puts things off: but, my dear Wolfgang, diarrhoea when one has a fever requires a doctor to know if the fever should be reduced or allowed to run its course as medicines designed to reduce the temperature cause an increase in diarrhoea: and if the diarrhoea is stopped at the wrong time, the *materia peccans* leads to gangrene. – God! We are in your hands.

Congratulations on the success of your symphony at the Concert Spirituel. I can imagine how anxious you

must have been.   Your determination to rush out into
the orchestra if things hadn't gone well was presumably
just a wild idea. God forbid! You must put this and all
such notions out of your head; they're ill considered, such
a step would cost you your life, which no man in his right
senses risks for a symphony. – Such an affront – and a
public affront to boot – would inevitably be avenged by
the sword not just by a *Frenchman* but by all who value
their honour. An Italian would say nothing but would lie
in wait at a street corner and shoot you dead. – From
Munich I've received reliable reports that Count Seeau
has been confirmed as intendant of music for Munich and
Mannheim; that a list of all the orchestral players has
been sent to Mannheim; that the two orchestras will be
combined and the worst players weeded out; Herr
Wotschitka and the other *valets de chambre* have been pen-
sioned off on a pension of 400 florins, *which surprises me*;
Dr *Sänfftel* had the effrontery to demand 3000 florins for
his treatment, whereupon he was stripped of his title and
salary; finally, it is hoped in Munich that the elector and
his wife, the electress, will be back in Munich with their
entire court by 10 August. – I began this letter with my
congratulations, – and Nannerl was planning to end it
with her own. But, as you can imagine, she's incapable
of writing a single word, now that she has to write – each
letter that she's supposed to write down brings a flood of
tears to her eyes. You, her dear brother, must take her
place, if – as we hope and desire – you can still do so.

But no! You can no longer do so – she has passed away – you are trying too hard to console me, no one is as eager as that unless driven to it quite naturally by the loss of all human hope or by the event itself. I'm now going to have some lunch, though I don't suppose I'll have much of an appetite.

I'm writing this at half past 3 in the afternoon. I now know that my dear wife is in heaven. I'm writing this with tears in my eyes but in total submission to God's will! Yesterday was the annual celebration of the dedication of the Holy Trinity, so our usual target practice was postponed till today. I was unable to cancel it at such a late hour and didn't want to either, in spite of your sad letter. We ate little, but Nannerl, who had cried a lot before lunch, was violently sick and had a terrible headache, so she went to lie down on her bed. Herr Bullinger and the rest of them found us in this deeply distressing situation. Without saying a word, I gave him your letter to read, and he acted his part very well and asked me what I thought of it. I told him that I was firmly convinced that my dear wife was already dead: he said that he was indeed inclined to suspect as much himself; and he then comforted me and as a true friend told me all that I had *already* told *myself*. I made an effort to cheer up and to remain so, while submitting to God's most holy will, we finished our target practice and everyone left, feeling very saddened, Herr Bullinger remained with me and, without appearing to do so, asked me if I thought that there was any hope in the condition that had been described to us. I replied that I thought that not only was she now dead but that she was already dead on the day you wrote your letter; that I had submitted to the will of God and had to remember *that I still had 2 children who I hoped would continue to love me inasmuch as I lived only for them*; that I was so firmly convinced that she was dead that I'd even written to you, reminding you to take care of her succession etc. To this he said, *yes, she's dead.* At that moment the scales fell from my eyes, scales that had been put in place by this sudden and unexpected turn of events, preventing me from seeing what had happened, for otherwise I'd have quickly suspected that you'd secretly written the truth to Herr Bullinger as soon as I'd read your letter. But your letter had really stunned me – at first I was too dumbfounded to be able to think properly. Even now I still don't know what to write! You don't need to worry about me; I shall play the man. But just think of your mother's tender love for you and you'll realize how much she cared for you just as when you reach maturity you'll love me more and more after my death – if you love me – *as I do not doubt* – you should take care of your health, – *my life depends on yours*, as does the future support of your sister, who honestly loves you with all her heart. It is unbelievably difficult when death severs a good and happy marriage, but you have to experience that for yourself to know it. – *Write and tell me all the details*; perhaps she wasn't bled enough? – – The only thing that's certain is that she trusted too much in herself and called in the doctor too late; meanwhile the inflammation of her intestines gained the upper hand. *Take good care of your health!* Don't make us all unhappy! Nannerl doesn't yet know about Bullinger's letter, but I've already prepared her to believe that her dear mother is dead. – Write to me soon – tell me everything – when she was buried – and where. – – Good God! To think that I'll have to go to Paris in search of my dear wife's grave! – We kiss you both with all our heart. I must close as the post is leaving. Your honest and utterly distraught father

Mozart

Make sure that none of your things are lost.